WEIGHT LOSS PSYCHOLOGY

LEARN EVERYTHING YOU NEED TO KNOW ABOUT LOSING BODY FAT NATURALLY, THANKS TO THE PSYCHOLOGICAL BASICS OF BURNING CALORIES

Jessy M. Brown

Table of Contents

Introduction..*4*

The power of the mind over the body............................*7*

    The importance of your mentality........................*10*

The visualization of your body..*14*

Set goals for eating right..*16*

    Set exercise goals..*18*

    Your body image..*23*

Hold on to your goals..*28*

    How to be consistent with your goals?..............*31*

Conclusion..*35*

Introduction

Weight loss is one of the goals of most men and women. If this is one of your dreams in life too, you have to be aware of the aspects that will help you achieve the results you expect. One of these aspects is his way of thinking. Without strong determination and a fixed mentality, successful weight loss results would be difficult to achieve.

First of all, changing your thinking is the first thing to consider when it comes to losing weight. Your weight loss plan won't succeed if you don't pay attention to the way you think. By telling yourself that you can't, you will surely fail and have a small chance to see the results. Therefore, you must think of these things upside down.

Instead of thinking negatively about weight loss, you should say that I will, that I can, and that I will succeed. You will have more confidence in telling yourself each of these things once you learn to change your way of thinking. To motivate yourself, you must know the value of motivation and how it can help you achieve your goals.

This is the main purpose of this book. With this guide, you will learn the true meaning of a mentality that can help you succeed and be more efficient in achieving your weight loss goals. It's important to change your way of thinking, and you have to realize the reasons why you have to consider it.

You are fortunate to find this book because it will provide you with ideas, details, tips and all about your thinking and your relationship and importance to weight loss.

With this guide, you can control your weight and learn everything you can do to reach your goals. Your journey to successful and satisfying weight loss is about to begin. Read on!

The power of the mind over the body

Your way of thinking plays a very important role in weight loss. What happens to you physically is only a reflection of the changes that occur within your system. So, you're what you think.

A person who aspires to lose their excess weight will experience changes in their blood pressure and heart rate. In the same way, the electrical conductivity of the skin and breathing reacts to your emotions and thoughts.

Maybe, you think you're too fat or you're not physically fit at all. If you are not happy, the stress will make your body feel in an unsafe state. This will result in the release of stress-causing hormones. When stressful thoughts and bad emotions are pursued, your body will become more tense. The stress-causing hormone, known as cortisol, has a big impact on your digestive system and your weight. Belly fat is one of the visible signs of stress.

➢ *How to lose your excess weight?*

The first thing you have to do is change your mind. When it comes to losing weight, you shouldn't think about a "diet. Instead, you should learn the best way to eat the foods you want. While doing so, you should think about nourishment rather than deprivation. Use mealtimes to enjoy the food served at the table. Mealtimes are the right time for you to forget the stressful problems or thoughts you have in life. In the long run, you will notice that you are enjoying eating and eating less food.

You must keep your body in a normal condition. Therefore, you have to find ways to stay fit and healthy. Eating foods that are helpful to your thinking is the best technique to eliminate stress and improve your health. This will allow you to achieve successful weight loss, even without dieting.

The importance of your mentality

Being closed-minded may be the reason you don't succeed in your long-term weight loss goals. Developing a good mentality is one of the most crucial things you must consider to achieve lasting change.

If you have a closed mind, you're the kind of person who tends to run away from challenges. In addition, you are likely to give up easily when you experience difficulties in achieving your goals. Although you are determined to change, everything is too hard for you. Therefore, you decide to stay within your comfort zone. You are determined to start taking steps to lose weight, but once you don't see the results as soon as possible, you prefer to give up and stop doing everything.

If you are open-minded and positive, you are always ready and courageous to face any challenge along your journey. You should expect obstacles to present themselves in your path, but when something bad happens, you should seek to deal with them using a strategy that will help you move in the positive direction.

When you are closed-minded, you tend to refrain from listening to the advice and suggestions of the people around you. You'll ignore those people's comments so you can stay on your current path. You also think that your efforts are useless because you know that you will not achieve it until the end.

An open-minded person is one who listens to what others can tell him or her. It also reflects their own thoughts, attitudes and actions. When you have this kind of mentality, you should take small steps forward. Having a positive mentality is equivalent to having emotional intelligence. You know that changes will never happen without her.

If you have a closed mind, you tend to look more at the physical aspect. You look at other people and you feel envy and jealousy because they are successful. You assume you can do better than them, but you don't do anything. Having a positive mentality, actions taken by others become your inspiration. You witness their accomplishments and learn by seeing what they do. You'll take that and find something that works for you.

As you can see, having a closed mind will never help you achieve the results you want. You will remain in your current state forever and will not notice developments and changes. You can't grow because you don't change your way of thinking or you don't do anything to overcome your negative thoughts.

When you open your mind and choose to do so, you will begin to see the changes that happen to you. Developments will be visible and you will begin to experience success. All this will come to your psychological method. If you struggle to lose fat and don't see the changes as you go through the cycle over and over again, read this book and think about what you can do to change the way you think.

The visualization of your body

Your thinking, whether positive or negative, can affect your body image. If you are trying to make changes in the shape of your body and the state of your health, you should start with your mind. The weight loss results you expect will be given to you once you have developed a proper body image. A well-developed body image seems to provide a blueprint of the exact look you'd like to achieve.

➢ *Why it's important*

Without making a change in your thinking, your thoughts about weight loss will be against the health routine or change you've started. You'll never find anything that works faster than your brain. Creating feelings and thoughts that support your body image will help you achieve the positive changes and results you want.

Today, most people seeking successful weight loss results rely on the numerous supplements available on the market. The truth is that weight loss results can also be achieved simply by having a positive mindset. By changing the way you think about weight loss and the way it happens, you're sure to get the results you expect. It will also allow you to change your whole life and maintain the new shape of your body.

Set goals for eating right

Metabolism is the process by which food consumed is processed and transformed into energy. The easiest way to understand this is to assume that food is gasoline for your body. Once your stomach empties, your body will begin to weaken and try to use the energy stored in your fat cells.

Some people who are trying to have a successful weight loss regimen limit their food intake, so they eat less than normal. On the other hand, this will never allow you to experience your goals, as your body will interpret reduced food intake as starvation, and will use fat cells as a survival mechanism for your body.

The most effective way to improve your metabolism and your body's ability to lose weight is to eat frequent small meals every day. Most people usually eat 2 to 3 times a day with large meals. To improve your metabolism, you should eat frequent small meals every day. You can eat at least 6 times a day with long intervals to give your body more time to digest the foods you eat.

By eating small meals every day, you will feel hungry and this can prevent your fats from being used against starvation. You should also eat more foods that are low in calories and fat, but high in fiber. These foods are the ones that will help you lose more and get better weight loss results. Avoid processed foods, especially those high in fat and sodium.

Once you change the way you think about food, it will be easier to change your usual eating habits. When you follow a particular weight-loss program, you should focus on your goal. You should not only lose weight, but also improve your health.

Set exercise goals

Being torn to shreds or sexy isn't hard to do if you mean it. What you have to do is change your mind. You know that exercise is important in weight loss and you have to be determined to do it every day. Here are some tips you can use to get the right mindset you need to be motivated to exercise regularly.

Regular exercise is known for the different health benefits it can provide. However, there are only a few people who lead an active lifestyle. If you want to improve your quality of life, you should start an exercise regimen. It will lower your blood pressure and may reduce your risk of various forms of cancer.

➢ *Here's how:*

1. Set realistic expectations - before starting your new exercise routine, you have to set your goal first. You have to be sure of what you'd like to accomplish. If this is the first time you've used an exercise regimen, you shouldn't get overwhelmed. You should focus on a small goal first and make a list containing the weight loss goals you would like to achieve. Once you set realistic expectations, it will be easier for you to reach them. After reaching the small goals you have, you can pursue your hard-to-reach goals. If you have a plan to join a fitness club, you may want to, as there are several gyms with personal trainers that can help you with your goals. If you don't really know what you would like to achieve, hiring these professionals may be the best solution to your problem. They will motivate you by making you understand the importance of concentrating on trying to lose more fat.

2. *Find a fitness partner* - to have more fun while exercising, you may want to find someone who is your fitness partner to go to the gym every day. Research shows that if you work together with someone, you will be motivated to do more in your exercise regimen. Whether you're having fun with someone while exercising or you become more competitive and able to push yourself, these things will depend on the type of personality you have.

3. Keep doing what you can - there's no need to worry if you don't have enough money to pay the gym fees. There is no rule that the exercise should be formal. You can simply go up and down the stairs 10 times a day. You can also take your dog for a walk outside, wherever he goes. Any action that can increase your heart rate is a type of cardiovascular exercise.

4. Eat nutritious and healthy foods - to be physically fit, you must pay attention to the foods you eat during your meals. You should have a well balanced and healthy diet which is a very crucial aspect when it comes to wealth and overall health. You can contact your dietitian if you need nutritional advice. He or she can tell you the right foods to eat and what would work best with your exercise regimen. Always keep in mind that exercise alone is not enough to achieve successful weight loss results. Exercise must be combined with a proper diet.

5. Have fun - you should never feel like you're the only person facing problems while trying to lose weight. Remember that there are millions of people around the world who face the same problem as you. Establishing the state of your mind is the initial step you need to take when it comes to exercising.

You should keep in mind that when you exercise, it is not to make your body feel tortured, but for its own good. This means that you should enjoy everything you are doing in your daily life. You can choose yoga as it is a great way to revitalize your mind as you become physically fit. If you are a man, you may want to join a basketball team where you will experience fun while your body begins to lose weight. You can also use free weights. If you start your new exercise regimen while having a negative mentality about exercise, you'll never be able to do it regularly. Always remember its importance.

Your body image

To achieve great weight loss results, you need to change the way you think. A great way to alter the way you think about exercise and your body image is to read and write affirmations every day. What are affirmations and how can they benefit you? Well, these are brief positive statements that you can read or write repeatedly when necessary. You can place them in the areas inside your home that you usually go to every day. By seeing them regularly, you'll have more confidence to face the challenges and start working harder to achieve better weight loss results.

Apart from the use of affirmations, you can also change your thinking with the use of other techniques:

- Consider the impact - you need to

think about how your own body image affects the other aspects of your life. You have to reflect on how your body image influences your work, your relationships and your whole self-image. You must determine whether or not this prevents you from achieving your goals. Try to think about how your body image negatively affects your life. Understanding that your body's dissatisfaction influences your life can be empowering. It's because knowing the problems will lead you to find solutions for them. Once you are aware of the effect of bad body images, you can start doing something to alleviate them.

- Look at yourself - most people complain about their thighs and their fatty stomachs. They have several questions that pertain to their failures to get the weight loss results they desire. If you are one of these people, you must be empowered so that you can see yourself fully. When you stand in front of the mirror, you should observe your whole

being and avoid worrying about your body parts.

   - Build a positive and good body image coming from within - most people depend on external factors that can break or cause their body images. When you read a magazine and see models with perfect bodies, you tend to doubt your appearance. Reading an Internet message about exercise and diet can make you feel worse. However, what will happen once you work with body image that can withstand external influences? You will definitely never find anything that is completely resistant, but you can do something that will turn your own body image into something stable. You can stand in front of the mirror and wait for negative thoughts to enter your mind. Once these thoughts arrive, you must imagine something that will protect you from them. Your thinking, your emotions and your heart rate will be protected by that. From here, your

positive mentality will come into play. That way, you'll be sure you're on the right track.

   - Change your way of thinking - when you change your way of thinking, you are enabling yourself to form a developed body image. When you have realized that losing weight is not the real goal you need to achieve, you are able to continue to have a good self-care routine. When you realize that diet plans aren't enough to get what you want, you concentrate on listening to what your body says. You may think that exercises are not really related to weight loss, but your body's movements can relieve stress.

   - Think of the positive attributes you have - when you have attractive eyes, you can publish something that will keep reminding you about your eyes. You can place this in the mirror inside the bathroom. They may face struggles as they reach their goals, but they are blessed to have those characteristics that

others do not.

Hold on to your goals

You always go to a gym, eat a balanced meal and spend enough hours sleeping, but you still don't feel well. You think you're not completely healthy. Today, most people are aware of the benefits they can get from staying healthy. However, most people don't spend time thinking about the most important aspect of weight loss control, and that is the mind.

You may be physically fit with exercise and a proper diet, but when your mentality is not in good shape, it may affect other areas of your life. The worst part is that it can keep you from achieving your goals. Everyday stress, depression, anxiety, and other psychological problems have become frequent. In 5 people, there is one who experiences psychological problems at some point in her life. This situation occurs because of negligence to pay attention to your mind.

➢ *The value of having a normal, positive mentality*

Scientific research has shown that bad mentalities overwhelmed by stress can trigger other health problems. Always keep in mind that having an unhealthy mentality can lead to an unhealthy physique. The disordered mentality can also retain a person. You can think about the obstacles to good health, better productivity at work, and better relationships. Find out the best way to deal with them.

By doing everything you can to stay in shape, you can also practice mind exercises, which can help reduce your negative emotions and thoughts. Ignore the negative thoughts that tell you useless things. Instead of thinking negatively, you should think on the other side. Tell yourself that you can do it and that you can make your dreams come true. Think of your negative thoughts as challenges and allow them to motivate you to try harder instead of giving up.

In the same way, you should practice gratitude and be grateful for the experiences and lessons taught throughout your life. Instead of thinking about your failures, you should always believe that bad things happen to teach you the right things and to help you recognize your mistakes. Thinking about the positive side of your circumstances will help you to have a positive mentality. When it comes to losing weight, you should concentrate on knowing the things that will cause you to fail and use them as motivation to become a positive thinker.

How to be consistent with your goals?

Most of the elements in life are helpful in achieving the results you expect when it comes to losing weight. On the other hand, the most important thing of all is your mind. If you want to lose weight and burn more fat, you have to condition your mind and believe in yourself that you can do whatever it takes to reach your goal.

Having a good and effective weight loss mentality will help you a lot. This will give you motivation and strength to face challenges. With these things, it will be easier for you to overcome the obstacles and temptations that may arise in your path. A good, positive weight loss mentality will help you promote long-term change and achieve a healthy, normal lifestyle.

If you are really serious about weight

loss and have already developed a positive mentality, you should look for ways to maintain it and the changes it can bring to your life. Here are some things you can do to keep up with the mentality changes you have:

  - *Remember about your goals* - to achieve complete and successful weight loss results, you must remember about the goals you want to achieve. You may want to write down all of your weight loss goals. To motivate your thinking, you must be specific about what you really want to accomplish. Make a fixed schedule of when you should see more changes. Make sure your goals are achievable and measurable. A considerable goal is one for which you can be held responsible. A good example of this is the loss of a specific percentage of fat that must be reached by a certain date.

  - *Think about your goals in your daily life* - you have to review all the goals you wrote in your journal, including the schedules. This is to make sure you're on the right track. You may wonder if the actions you took for a specific day brought you closer to or away from your aspirations.

- Aim for smaller, shorter goals - you can divide the long-term goals you have into smaller, manageable goals. This way, you will find that they are less difficult to do, so you will be more motivated to keep your positive mentality in achieving the continuous changes that occur inside and outside of your body. Instead of thinking you have to lose 50 pounds within a year, you should concentrate on losing one pound each week because it's easier to achieve. In this way, your change of mentality will go further.

- Alter your focus - you have to forget the negative aspects of weight loss. These aspects include the feeling of deprivation. Instead of worrying about them, you should focus your attention on the positive aspects of weight loss. You can pay

attention to how your clothes look and how your body will react to them.

*- **Think more about being healthy** -* you shouldn't obsess over your dream of losing weight. You should pay attention to improving your health that will improve your quality of life. You have to eat foods that will improve your health instead of foods that are primarily intended for weight loss.

Conclusion

Like what is discussed in the previous chapters, in this last chapter we would like to remind you of the importance of having a good mentality. When it comes to goals, whether it's about weight loss or not, you'll see that changing your mindset is the first and most important aspect that will lead you to success. When it comes to losing weight, how can a change in mentality benefit you?

Seeking to change the way you think about weight loss will give you several advantages, including:

- Having a positive mentality will make you feel more confident - to be physically fit, you have to put your mind in order and forget the usual way you see weight loss. Changing your thinking is the first step to an effective weight loss management plan. Without a strong will and determination brought by positive thinking, it will be harder for you to get what you want. When you change your mind, you'll feel more confident and be able to meet the challenges of maintaining the weight that's right for you. In weight loss, possession of a positive mentality must be persistently maintained. This will give you more confidence to maintain the results you enjoy today throughout your life.

- Changing your thinking will lead to a normal health condition - when you change the negative way you think about weight loss, you will find that achieving overall health is easier to achieve. Changing the way you think will not only help you succeed in your weight loss plan, it will also indicate a healthier way of life.

- Changing your way of thinking will allow you to become an optimistic person - you should change your way of thinking and you have to become a

positive thinker if you are really sincere about how to achieve a more attractive physique. Changing your mind's usual environment and beliefs when it comes to losing weight will help you be optimistic. Optimism is a good attitude you must have to lose weight. Did you know that what your mind can conceive, your body can achieve?

- Changing your way of thinking will make you feel good - when you say you have to change your way of thinking, this means you have to forget your negative attitudes like pessimism, as it will keep you away from success. If you really want to lose weight in a healthy and safe way, you have to tell yourself that you can do it. However, words alone are not enough to help you reach your goals. So be sure to have patience and determination. Did you know that these are two of the main keys that will help you achieve a dramatic change in your body?

All these are the benefits you can get

when your thinking has changed. As you can see, choosing to change your usual way of thinking will help you get more, apart from the weight loss results you expect. So, what are you waiting for? You should begin your struggle to change your thinking before taking the other steps in your weight loss management plan. Keep in mind that weight loss can best be achieved when you focus on your mental rather than your physical appearance. No matter what happens, your mind is still the boss. Keep these things in mind and you'll make sure you're successful. It may not be an easy path, but it certainly can be achieved, especially if you put into practice the advice this book has given you. I wish you the best of luck and remember that everything is possible!

Now yes, I wish you the best in your results, and remember, everything is practical; theory without action is of no use to you.

A big hug, your friend, Jessy!

By the way, when you achieve your results little by little, I highly recommend you, if you want to learn much more about methods of losing weight, my book on "HOW TO MAKE THE CETOGENIC DIET WITHOUT STOP EATING", is a book that I'm sure will help you a lot on your way to "good health".

Without further ado, you can find it in the Amazon search engine, like: "How to do the ketogenic diet without stopping eating" or looking for my name, like: "Jessy M. Brown"... Once again I wish you success in your results!